Indians of the Great Plains

Preface

Most people think of the Indians of the Great Plains when they think about American Indians, for these were the people who followed the buffalo, wore elegantly beaded and decorated clothing, rode painted ponies, and lived in graceful tipis. This lifestyle came only after the introduction of the horse by the Spanish, two centuries ago.

The principal tribes of the Great Plains include the:

- Arapaho
- Blackfeet
- Cheyenne
- Comanche
- Crow
- Hidatsa
- Iowa
- Kansa
- Kiowa
- Mandan

- Missouri
- Omaha
- Osage
- Pawnee
- Plains Apache
- Plains Cree
- Plains Ojibwa
- Shoshone (Snake)
- Sioux (Lakota, Dakota, Nakota)
- Wichita

Each of these tribes has its own language, culture, traditions, and lifestyle.

The arrival of the whites to the Central Plains was disastrous for the Indians living there. Many of them died within a few years of diseases (measles, tuberculosis, cholera, and small pox) brought by the white man. The Mandans, for example, who farmed in small villages in what is now North and South Dakota, lost more than ninety percent of their people.

During the late 1800's, it was thought that all the Indians would soon be dead. For a time it seemed their cultures would be lost forever. In the past half century the numbers of Plains people have begun to grow again. We now know how very rich the culture of the Plains Indians was. This thematic unit contains cross-cultural activities which show some aspects of how the Indians of the Great Plains lived during the buffalo days.

Activity:
Have students work in pairs or groups. Choose a Plains Tribe from the list above to report on. Using the report form on the following page, have students complete some simple research to introduce them to the various Plains Indians.

Report On _____
A Great Plains Indian Tribe

Their name means _____

```
|                                              |
|                                              |
|                                              |
|                                              |
|                                              |
|            A Drawing of their home           |
```

The Men:

_____

_____

_____

_____

The Women:

_____

_____

_____

_____

They believed:

They ate:

_____ _____

_____ _____

_____ _____

_____ _____

_____

Prepared by:_____

Bibliography

Folk tales and Legends

Folk tales of the Native Americans by Dee Brown, Henry Holt and Company, 1993.

Her Seven Brothers by Paul Goble, Bradbury Press, 1988.

    *Paul Goble has written a number of books about the Plains Indians and their legends; check your library or children's book stores.

Myths and Legends of the Sioux by Marie L. McLaughlin, University of Nebraska Press, 1990.

Quillworker, A Cheyenne Legend by Terri Cohlene, Watermill Press, 1990.

The Legend of Scarface, A Blackfeet Indian Tale by Robert San Souci, Doubleday, 1978.

The Legend of Scarface at Blackfeet Indian Tale by Robert San Souci, Doubleday, 1978.

Wigwam Evenings by Charles A. Eastman (Ohiyesa) and Elaine Goodale Eastman, University of Nebraska Press, 1990.

Where the Buffaloes Begin by Olaf Baker, Puffin Books, 1985.

Of Interest to Teachers

Bury My Heart at Wounded Knee by Dee Brown, Henry Holt and Company, 1970.

Canyons by Gary Paulsen, Dell, 1990.

Keepers of the Earth by Joseph Bruchac, Fifth House Publishers, 1991.

Morning Girl by Michael Dorris, Hyperion Books for Children, 1992.

    (Not about Plains Indians, but appropriate)

Native American Animal Stories by Joseph Bruchac, Fulcrum Publishing, 1992.

Quest for Courage by Rodolph Stormy, Roberts Rinehart Publishers, 1993.

The Indian Heritage of America by M., Jr., Alfred A. Knopf, 1968.

The Native Americans: An Illustrated History by David Hurst Thomas, Turner Publishing, 1993.

Through Indian Eyes by Beverly Slapin and Doris Seale, New Society Publishers, 1992.

Thunder Rolling in the Mountains by Scott O'Dell, and Elizabeth Hall, Yearling, 1992.

When Thunders Spoke by Virginia Driving Hawk Sneve, University of Nebraska Press, 1974.

Where the Broken Heart Still Beats by Carolyn Meyer, Gulliver Books, 1992.

Procession

The river of people flowed down through the valley,

dust billowing up almost hiding the grandeur.

Old chiefs walked ahead,

scouts and sentries far outside,

protecting women on ponies,

dragging travoises, carrying cradle boards

and tipis

children play

moving alongside.

I watched you stop three times

and thought take me with you the next time you go.

I want to go with you,

I want to stop with you,

I want to sit with you and drink of your soup.

When you halted a fourth time I ran to catch up,

but you melted into mist,

a vanishing vision.

Where could you have gone

with your beauty and grace?

Gone the buffalo days,

Gone forever.

— Mari Lu Robbins

Note: This activity may be done as a whole class brainstorming session or in cooperative learning groups.
Combine all the information to create a large chart to leave up in class throughout the unit of study.
Update the chart as the unit progresses.

Before We Begin

What we know about the Indians of the Great Plains	What we want to learn about the Indians of the Great Plains

What Indians Held Most Sacred

The Indians of North America nurtured the continent for forty thousand years before the coming of the white man. They were different in many ways, but they all had values which guided their movements and religion which guided their lives.

THEY BELIEVED THAT...

THE EARTH IS SACRED.

The Indians see the universe as being under the care and direction of a supreme power. Sometimes that power is called Wakan Tonka, the Great Mystery, the Everywhere Power, or the Great Spirit. The supreme power created the earth and its creatures for the use of humans. In return, it is necessary for humans to treat the animals, earth, and plants which feed and shelter them with great respect. Everything the Indian does is to honor and revere this supreme power.

EVERY PART OF CREATION HAS A SPIRIT.

Every plant, rock, stream, wind, animal, bird, fish, insect, moon, sun, and star has its own spirit. Because of these beliefs, there are many myths and legends about the relationship between humans and animals. One can never think of oneself ahead of another, for that would break the circle of life.

ALL MEMBERS OF THE TRIBE HAVE A SPECIAL PLACE.

Women are honored as the life bearers. Only with them can the tribe continue. They are hardworking and take great pride in building and maintaining beautiful lodges, preserving and preparing good meals, and making beautiful clothing.

Children are a gift from the supreme being, and because of this they are loved and carefully trained and taught. Indian parents almost never punish a child. Children are taught to admire the most honorable adults in the tribe. Every adult is a teacher for every child.

Old people are revered as having gained great wisdom in their long lives. Usually, they live in the same lodge with the family and serve as teachers and advisers for the children. No old person will go hungry as long as there is food.

Activity

Discussion questions to develop awareness of one's own values.

1. What can we do to treat the earth with respect?
2. Are older people today treated as the Indians treated them?
3. Do people ever contribute to an animal or plant becoming extinct?

What the People Did All Day

The Indian people of the Great Plains knew exactly what each person in the tribe had to do every day because their customs told them that men did certain things, and women did certain things. Every adult was a teacher for every child, and children were taught from a very early age what they would do as adults.

Each of the jobs filled by the Plains Indian people was important to their way of life, and each of them was honored by the people. The greatest accomplishment of a man and woman was to raise children who were brave, generous, and who fulfilled their responsibilities well. Before the white people came to change their whole world, the strong traditions of the people gave them a great deal of security, so each person always knew what was expected of him or her.

Men

Men filled the very dangerous roles of hunters, warriors, and protectors of the tribe. Hunting was a necessity, and it was a dangerous job. Buffalo can weigh as much as four thousand pounds and are easily frightened and stampeded.

The man's job of warring could easily claim his life. When a band of people was traveling from one place to another, as they did to follow the buffalo and to find grass for their horses, the warriors and scouts rode all around the people in order to protect them from dangers such as attacking warriors or wild animals.

On days when the tribe stayed in one place, the men made the tools they needed for hunting and warring. They made their own bows, arrows, shields, and lances. Men also had many ceremonial and religious duties.

No man could marry until he had proven himself to be a good hunter and brave in war. For a man to become a chief he had to show many times that he was brave and a good provider. A chief was expected to be generous and helpful to others.

Women

Women were honored and protected as the life-givers of the tribe. Their duties centered around the home and the family. Raising children was necessary for the tribe to survive, and it was important that the traditions and customs be taught to the children.

After the men hunted the buffalo, the women butchered, cooked, and preserved the meat. They gathered wild berries, fruits, and roots which they dried. They fleshed and tanned hides, and they sewed all the clothing and moccasins for the family. Women owned the tipis, so they made them and took care of them. Women also owned many horses, sometimes as many as the men.

Women occasionally became warriors, and many of the Plains tribes had stories about women who had gone to war. Although women did not become chiefs, they had much power and influence in the tribe through their husbands.

Children

School for a Plains Indian child began the day he or she was born. The infant was taught not to cry because a crying child would endanger the whole tribe by letting an enemy know they were present. Throughout their childhood, children learned the many duties and skills they would be responsible for as adults. The boys learned to be hunters and warriors, and the girls learned to be homemakers.

Children were told the stories of how and why their traditions came to be, how the world was made, and their relationship with the earth and its creatures. They learned all the stories by heart, so when they were grown they would be able to pass the stories on. Many of the stories were taught to the children by the grandparents who lived in the family lodge.

Children's toys were miniatures of the things they would use as adults. Little girls carried dolls in small, beaded cradle boards. After a move, they set up their own little tipis. Boys learned to hunt birds, rabbits, or prairie dogs with small bows and arrows. The children often moved in their own band alongside the main band. When the tribe was on the move, they pretended to do what they saw their parents doing.

Note: This activity can be completed as a whole group activity, as a small group activity, or individually.

Directions:
In space A below, write the jobs Indian men are expected to do. In space C, write the jobs women were expected to do. In space B write the jobs which are shared.

Venn Diagram: Jobs

Jobs

life-giver

hunter

teacher

worshiper

cook

respecter of nature

hardworking

preserver of food

warrior

protector

horse owner

sewer

owner of tipis

owner of horses

chiefs

tanned hides

tool maker

Can you think of any more?

A

B

C

The Earth Lodge

It's often thought that all the Indians of the Great Plains were nomads living in tipis and following the buffalo herds. Some groups, such as the Cheyenne and the Sioux, did live that way, but others lived most of the year in villages of earth lodges. The Pawnee lived in large, round, dome-shaped houses of wood and earth. The main living areas were partly underground.

An earth lodge was constructed around a circular floor by setting strong posts in a circle about ten feet from each other outside the circle. Beams were laid on the tops of these posts from one post to the next, then four very large strong posts were set in a square in the center of the circle. Heavy beams connected the tops of these four posts, and long poles were laid from the outside beams to those in the center. This provided a framework which was covered by willow branches, grass thatch, and shingles of sod and earth. Saplings were laid across the spaces between the four central posts, with a hole left for a chimney.

A rectangular entranceway led into the lodge. Two pieces of buffalo hide served as doors. A fireplace was dug in the center of the lodge. This was surrounded by flat rocks.

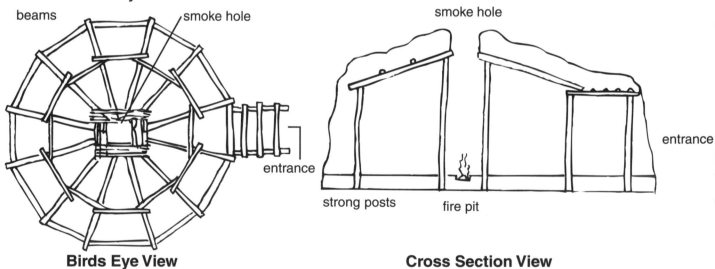

Birds Eye View

Cross Section View

The earth lodges were very strong, and provided good shelter from rain and cold. An earth lodge usually lasted ten years. Men and women worked together to build the lodges.

Make a Table-Top Tipi

The groups of Plains Indians that were nomadic lived in tipis. Tipis were made out of animal skins. It was the job of the Indian woman to put it up and take it down. She could do it in about an hour. Tipis were decorated inside and out. A fire placed near the back of the tipi allowed the smoke to flow out through a hole at the top.

Create a whole village of these easy-to-make tipis.

Materials for each tipi:
• one half of a large flour tortilla (Do not use lowfat tortillas.)
• 4 bamboo skewers cut to 7" (18 cm) lengths (Leave the ends pointed.)
• 3 toothpicks
• food coloring mixed in water
• paintbrush or cotton swab

Steps to follow:
1. Fold the tortilla into a cone shape.
2. Thread toothpicks through the edges to hold it closed.
3. Thread skewers through the bottom and out through the top of the cone-shaped tortilla.
4. Decorate the outside by painting designs with colored water.

These handy little tipis will turn very hard overnight and last forever.

The Buffalo: A Walking Commissary

The buffalo was a necessity for the Plains Indians. The buffalo was hunted because it was good to eat, rich in protein, and there were millions of them.

This animal provided over seventy different items for food, shelter, and clothing. All parts of the buffalo were used. Nothing was wasted. Because the buffalo was so essential, it also became the center of many of the Indian's religious ceremonies and legends.

The word list below tells some uses for buffalo. Discuss them and decide what part of the buffalo each one came from. Write them in the appropriate box on the next page.

arrowhead	meat
tipi covers	clothes
awls	blanket
flyswatter	paintbrush
jerky	saddles
whips	liver
cups	fat
padding/stuffing	snowshoes
war clubs	game counters
tongue	bowstrings
spoons	drums
robes	scraper
brains	moccasins
fire carriers	shields
knives	masks

Plains Indians EMC 545

How the Buffalo Was Used

FLESH AND ORGANS	BONES AND HORNS

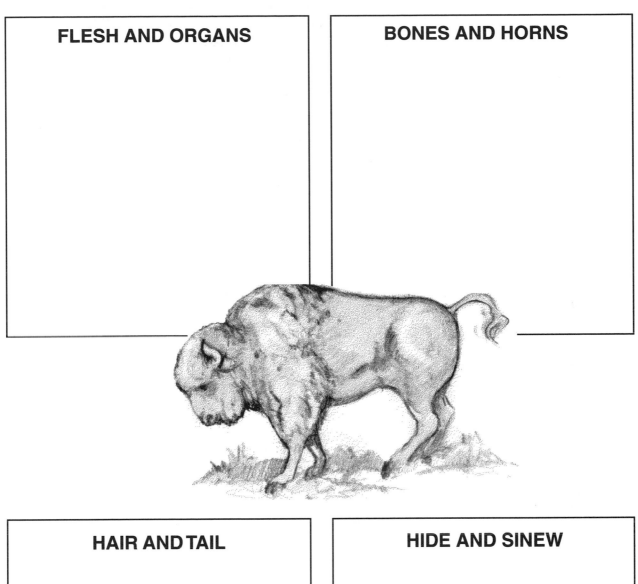

HAIR AND TAIL	HIDE AND SINEW

15

The Parfleche: Kitchen Cabinet of the Plains

One of the most useful items made from buffalo hides by Plains Indian women was the parfleche. It was sturdy and tough, and it usually was beautifully painted. A large parfleche could contain much dried meat or pemmican to be saved for winter food.

A parfleche is easy to make. Follow the directions below to make one of your own.

Materials:
- large brown grocery bag
- scissors
- pencil
- ruler
- hole punch
- piece of yarn 15" (38 cm)

Steps to follow:
1. Cut bottom off large brown grocery bag. Throw away bottom.
2. Cut down one side of remaining bag and lay flat.
   Trim to approximately 14" x 36" (36 x 91 cm).
3. Measure 2 inches (5 cm) in on the two long sides. Fold in.
4. Measure 11 inches (28 cm) in from right side.
   Fold left side to the mark. Fold right side over left.
5. Punch two holes about 1inch (2.5 cm) in from the end of right side.
   Close both flaps.
6. Using a pencil, mark through punched holes to paper layer underneath.
   Punch these holes in left flap only.
7. Open parfleche. Thread yarn through two bottom holes.
   Tie a knot so yarn does not become loose.
8. Now thread yarn through the two top holes and tie loosely to hold it closed.
9. Decorate the right and left folds with Indian designs.

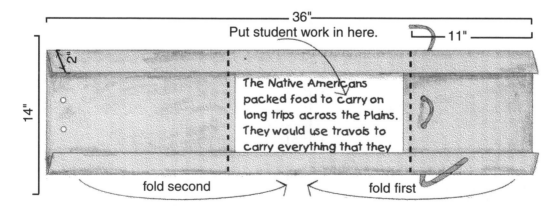

Students can keep all their important Indian papers in this handy folder.

Plains Indians EMC 545

Indian Maps

Did you know that the Indians drew their own maps? They made maps to show the direction and purpose of a certain route to be taken by someone.

This map shows a fur trader where to go to trade.

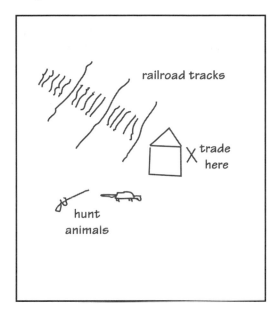

This map shows where a war party attacked an enemy and where they stopped.

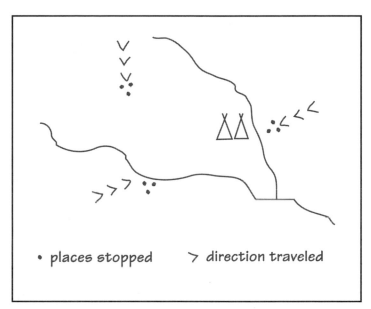

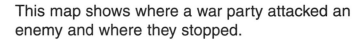

Study this map. Write your own ideas about what it is showing.

_____

_____

_____

_____

_____

_____

_____

North American Indian Groups

This map shows the locations of groupings of North American Plains Indians. The tribes in these groupings are thought to be related to each other because they share language families and lifestyles.

Activity:
Get a map of the United States and Canada on which states and provinces are labeled. On the map below, label the states and provinces to show where the different Plains Indians lived. Color each state.

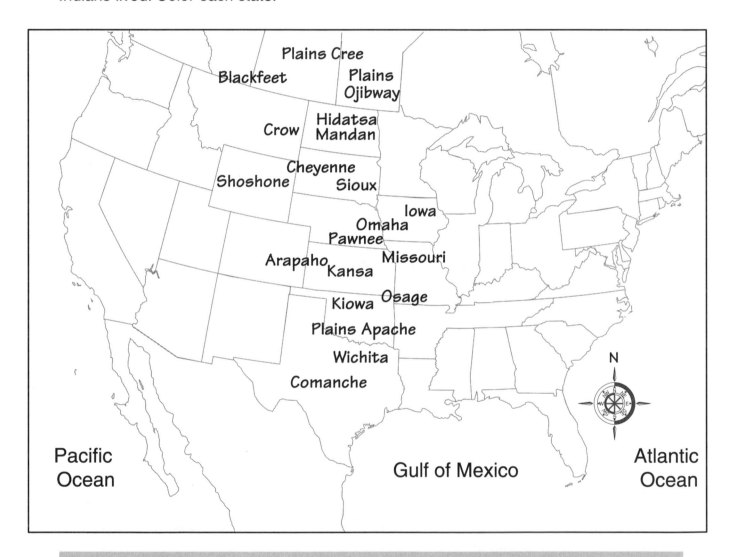

Discussion questions:
1. Have you ever visited one of the states you colored? What do you remember about it?
2. Is where you live similar to or different from the Plains Indians part of America? How?

Winter Counts

The Plains Indians did not have calendars as we know them, but they had an interesting method of keeping track of time. Instead of numbering years, they remembered "winters" by a particular event or situation which occurred during that winter.

The winter count would have been painted on buffalo hide. The one below shows events which happened over three years. These counts were carefully saved and referred to.

Activity: Make your own winter count.
• On the buffalo hide below, make one mark for every winter of your life.
• Draw a symbol to represent an event you feel to be the most important event of that year for you.
• You may need to ask a parent or other adult in your life for help.

Disappearance of Indian Lands

These maps show how quickly land which was promised to the Indians "for as long as the rivers shall flow and the grass shall grow" was taken from them by the government. When the white men came to North America, all of the continent belonged to the Indians. By 1850 almost half of it had been taken away, and by 1880 about ninety percent had been taken. Now only the very poorest lands in the country belong to the Indians as reservations.

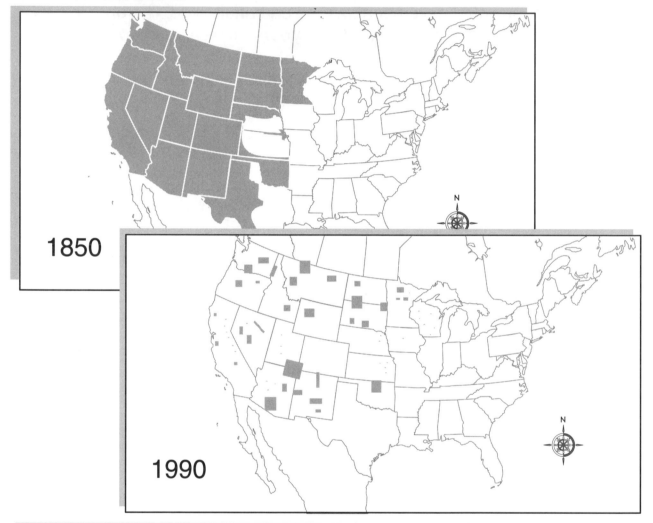

1850

1990

ACTIVITY: The time line on the following page will show you how long Indians have been in North America.

- Fill in the scale: 1 cm equals 1,000 years.
- Carefully make a mark every centimeter on the time line.
- On the arrow pointing left write B.C.
- On the arrow pointing right write A.D.
- Label the first mark on top line 40,000 B.C. "First Americas came to North America."
- Label the second mark to the right of the dotted line "2000 A.D."
- Label the last mark on the bottom line "2000 A.D."
- Label 1492 A.D. "First European explorers."
- Label current year.

Paste here

Native American

scale: ⌐_ = 1 cm = _____

Cut here

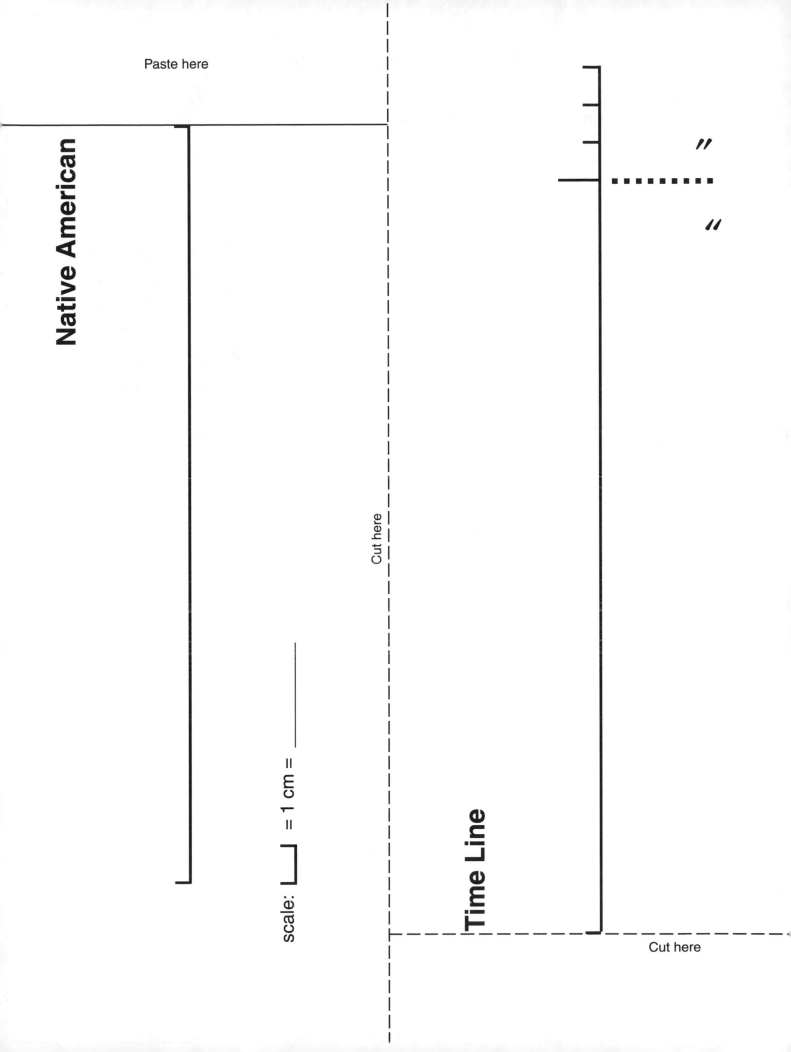

"

"

Time Line

Cut here

War and Peace Chiefs

Sitting Bull

Sitting Bull was a Sioux Indian Chief. He was born in 1831. As a boy he was called Hunk-es-ni, or Slow, because he was so careful in everything he did. He killed his first buffalo when he was ten. At fourteen he won his first battle honor. He painted his pony red and himself yellow, followed the enemy, a Crow, and struck him with his coup stick and then galloped safely away. He was allowed to adopt his father's name, "Sitting Bull." His reputation as a warrior grew. Soon his people felt the pressure of the white man's advance onto the Plains. Sitting Bull refused to attend peace talks or sign any treaties. In 1876 he defeated George Custer in The Battle of Little Bighorn (also known as "Custer's Last Stand"). Sitting Bull and his followers fled to Canada, but they returned in 1881. He became a celebrity, traveling with Buffalo Bill's Wild West Show. He continued to encourage the Sioux to refuse to sell their land. He died in 1890 when he was killed by Indian police for allegedly resisting arrest.

Red Cloud

Red Cloud was a chief of the Oglala Sioux Indians. He was born in 1822. As a boy he trained himself to run for hours without stopping, to go for days without food, and to stay awake all night. He proved his worth in battle many times and became famous for his good luck. He was also known as Medicine Man. He led opposition to the Bozeman Trail through Indian lands in Colorado and Montana. The Indians thought the Bozeman Trail was a threat to their hunting grounds. They were angered by the white man's intrusion and vowed to shut down the trail.

"The Great Spirit raised me in this land, and it belongs to me,"
Red Cloud had said.
"The white man was raised over the great waters, and his land is over there.
Since they crossed the sea, I have given them room.
There are now white people all about me.
I have but a small spot of land left.
The Great Spirit told me to keep it."

His opposition led to the trail being left alone. Red Cloud later lived in peace with the whites but was no longer a chief. He died in 1909, an old man.

Make a Triptych

Materials for each triptych:
- 6" x 18" (15 x 46 cm) white construction paper
- ruler
- 3 pieces of 5" x 5" (13 cm) lined paper
- pencil and crayons

Steps to follow:
1. Make a mark at 6"(15 cm) and 12"(30.5 cm) on the long edge of the construction paper.
2. Fold at these marks so the paper is divided into three equal parts.
3. Draw a vertical line about 1"(2.5 cm) from the bottom of the paper through all three squares. This represents the land.
4. Imagine yourself as a Plains Indian.
5. In the first space, draw yourself and your family hunting buffalo.
6. In the second space, draw yourself and your family living in a tipi.
7. In the third space, draw yourself having fun or relaxing.
8. On the lined paper, write a paragraph describing what is happening in each picture.
9. Attach completed paragraphs to the back of each picture.

How People Got Their Names

Plains Indian children were named soon after they were born, but most of them, particularly boys, received new names later. Sometimes a name was given to recognize something about how the person looked or acted. A child who ate a lot might be named "Eats Plenty." Sitting Bull, the famous Sioux chief, was named "Slow" as a child because of his way of looking closely at food placed in his hand before he began to eat it.

Sometimes a child or young adult might be named after a person who had lived a long and successful life. Other names might be given because of some unusual happening. A young warrior who was once followed by a magpie when he went on the warpath one time was named "Mysterious Magpie." Cheyenne women usually kept the name they were given as a child, while a man might change his name two, three, or even four times during his life.

The giving of a name was a serious event because it was believed the name would affect the person's life. Plains Indians believed all words were powerful, but names were the most powerful words of all.

When a child was to be named, the parents would invite several respected older men and women to a feast in their lodge. The mother would hand the child to an elder and ask that person to pray for the child and ask the powers above to help the child grow into a good person. The elder would then hold the child and pray for it.

It's All in a Name

- Write your entire name on the line below using bold letters.
- Interview a parent to find out why you received each of your names.
- Write the reasons in a paragraph below the line.

_____

_____

_____

_____

_____

- Imagine yourself a Plains Indian child.
- Think of your strengths and choose a name that describes you.
- Write your new name on the line below using bold letters.
- Write the reasons for your new name in a paragraph below the line.

_____

_____

_____

_____

_____

Make a Mandala

Native American mandalas are beautiful items. They are made from hoops, beads, suede, feathers, and white wool.

Materials for each mandala:
- metal or wooden hoop (rounded coat hanger will work)
- suede lacing
- colored feathers
- colored beads
- white cotton wool cut into 12" (30 cm) lengths
- circular piece of suede or leather 3" (8 cm) diameter smaller than the hoop
- tape
- hole punch

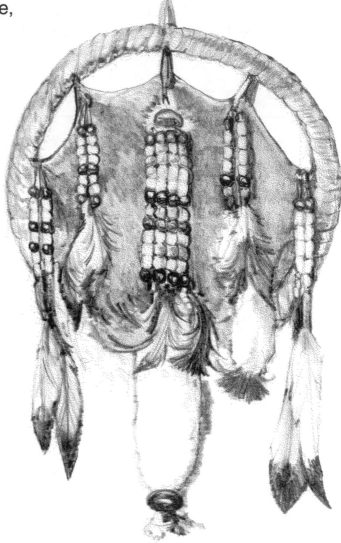

Steps to follow:
1. Tape end of suede lacing to hoop and wrap closely without twisting. Tape end.
2. Punch holes 1/2" (1 cm) apart evenly around suede circle.
3. Attach suede circle to hoop using suede lacing as shown.
4. String beads and feathers on ends of suede lacing.
5. Tie cotton wool onto the bottom of the hoop.
6. Decorate with beads or tie with lacings strung with pony beads.

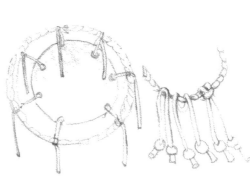

The Diet of the Plains Indians

The Plains Indians' diet consisted largely of meat. They also ate many wild fruits, nuts, and berries in addition to meat. Wild turnips, potatoes, and other roots and greens were favorite foods which they added to soups. Wild herbs were picked and used for flavoring and for medicines.

Meat was not always easy to get. Hunting was a difficult and dangerous job. Many days might pass between the times when wild game was available. A hunter often ate the raw liver of an animal as soon as he killed it. Its high nutritive value gave him strength to butcher the meat and carry it back to the people.

Soup: A Favorite food of the Plains Indians

Where ever the Indians roamed, a pot of soup was put over the fire. They would put meat, bones, and water into a clean animal stomach or bladder. This container was then hung on four upright sticks which were stuck securely into the ground. Clean stones were heated in a fire until very hot and then put into the water. As the water boiled, it cooked the meat and any plants which had been added. Hot soup would be ladled out into bone cups.

Vegetable Soup

Ingredients: beef stock
vegetables: onions, celery, potatoes, carrots
optional: a handful of barley, rice, beans, or macaroni
salt and pepper to taste

Directions: Cook in a large pot on top of the stove on low heat for two or three hours, or use a slow cooker for 4 or more hours.

Enjoy!

Tip: The longer soup cooks, the better it tastes!

The Three Sisters:
Corn, Beans, and Squash

Three of the most well-loved American crops, in addition to potatoes, tomatoes, and melons, are the ones the Indians called "The Three Sisters": corn, beans, and squash of all kinds.

Many of the Indians of the Great Plains did not plant crops, except for a little tobacco, eating wild fruits and berries instead. But others did plant crops, including the Pawnees, Rees, Mandans, Hidatsas, and Plains Apaches. The Three Sisters were the most popular vegetables to plant because they were so versatile. Not only could they be eaten fresh, but they could also be dried for future use, and corn could be ground into flour for making bread.

Try the following recipe for corn chowder.

Corn Chowder

Ingredients:
1 medium onion, chopped
2 cans creamed corn
1 can whole kernel corn, drained
1 cup (250 ml) diced potatoes, cooked until tender
2 1/2 cups (625 ml) milk
1/2 (2 ml) teaspoon salt
pepper to taste

Directions:
1. In a large saucepan brown onions, cooking over low heat.
2. Add remaining ingredients and bring to a boil, then turn down the heat and simmer for a few minutes.

Mm-mm-good!

       Plains Indians EMC 545

Preserving Meat

Meat was the most important part of the Plains Indian diet. The people learned ways to preserve their meat for times when no fresh meat was available.

They used a very simple process for drying meat. They cut it into very thin strips and hung it across sinew lines or wooden racks to dry. This jerky was used for making soups. Wild plants were added when they were available.

Sometimes the dried meat was pounded into a powder and mixed with dried, pounded berries and melted fat. This became a favorite food called pemmican, which could also be carried on trips or stored for winter. Meat preserved this way could be stored for years.

Making Jerky

Ingredients and supplies:

• lean round steak
• salt
• liquid smoke
• flat baking pan
• baking rack

Steps to follow:

1. Trim fat and cut lean round steak into strips.
2. Sprinkle the strips with salt and liquid smoke.
3. In the baking pan, place one layer of meat strips, then place another layer in the opposite direction.
4. Continue layering the rest of the meat.
5. Cover and set it in the refrigerator overnight.
6. In the morning, drain the strips and pat them dry with paper towels.
7. Move the strips to a baking rack.
8. Put into the oven at 250 degrees Fahrenheit (120 degrees Celsius).
9. Bake for about three and a half hours or until the meat is dry.

The Importance of Myths and Legends for the Indians of the Great Plains

Myths and legends were the stories which told how and why everything was to be done in a certain way, and they were told to every child. Any disaster which came to any of the people was proof that someone had disobeyed the laws which all knew to be true. Every success was proof that the way one was living was the correct way to live. Going against the way of the people was a sure road to disaster, the breaking of the "hoop" of life. Following the way of the people led to harmony and happiness, because it allowed life to flow in a continuous circle without end.

Myths and legends told these things about our world:

How the world came to be.
How humans and other creatures came to be.
How humans are related to the other creatures of the world.
Why it is important to do things a certain way.
Why some things are bad and some things are good.
The consequences of doing what is right.
The consequences of doing what is wrong.

Write Your own Legend

Fill in the blanks below to give you an outline for your legend.

Name an animal _____

List a special feature of that animal _____

Imagine what the animal looked like before it had this special feature

_____

Imagine a way that animal received that feature _____

Imagine an obstacle that might get in its way _____

How did the animal overcome the obstacle?_____

Now you are ready to write your own legend.

A Little Book About Sweet Medicine

To the Teacher:

The Indians of the Great Plains often had complex mythologies to explain to them the origins of their traditions, ceremonies, and religious beliefs. In this legend, the Cheyenne culture hero Sweet Medicine first shows his people that he has supernatural powers by being able to cut off his head and put it back on, and by commanding the winds to blow. When he does this, he earns the credibility he needs to show the people how to manage the important aspects of their lives, such as warfare and marriage.

Use this mini-book to introduce or review information about the importance of myth and legend in the traditions of the Plains Peoples.

Reproduce pages 31, 32, 33, 34 for each student. Cut the pages in half and put them in order. Staple the pages along the left side. Have students draw detailed illustrations to go with the text on each page. The pictures will be drawn on the back of the previous page. When the book is open, the page on the left is an illustration to go with the text on the right. Color the illustrations brightly.

Discuss the lessons Sweet Medicine taught his people.

Sweet

Medicine

Teaches

the People

Long ago, when the people first came to this place, Sweet Medicine was born to a Cheyenne family. From the very beginning, he was a special child. He was very intelligent, and while he was still a baby, he understood what people were saying. When he was still young, he wore a robe made of a yellow buffalo hide with the hair side out and the head still on. The robe was made from a buffalo calf which his father had hunted just for him. When he grew older, he wore the robe of the black, two-year-old buffalo which his father also hunted just for him.

When Sweet Medicine was seventeen years old, he told his father, "The spiritual elders are going to have a medicine dance. I am going to this dance."

His father said, "Son, the men who attend this dance must show the people their power. What power do you have? You are still just a boy?"

Sweet Medicine's said, "I will cut off my head with my bowstring, and you will put it back on as I tell you."

Sweet Medicine's father painted him red all over and put an eagle feather in his hair. They went to the medicine dance together, and when the people saw them, everyone said, "Look! Sweet Medicine is coming!"

"My son wishes to dance," Sweet Medicine's father said. The music began, and Sweet Medicine danced. Even though he was the youngest, he was the best dancer there. As he danced, he kept time by rubbing his bowstring back and forth across his neck.

Suddenly his head fell from his body, the eyes still open and looking at the people. His body remainded standing, and everyone was very frightened.

"Sweet Medicine cut off his head!" they called out to each other. They sat down, not knowing what to do.

Sweet Medicine's father took his body and lay it on the ground. He put the head in place pointing toward the rising sun. Then he covered his son with a robe. In a little while, Sweet Medicine stood up and faced the rising sun. He shook his robe toward the sun four times, and on the fourth time, the wind blew down from the north.

"Look!" the people said, "Sweet Medicine has called the north wind!" And the people all feasted, because Sweet Medicine had shown them his power.

Sweet Medicine lived to be a very old man, much older than anyone else has ever lived. While he was alive, he taught the people all the laws they were to follow.

He taught young men not to marry until they had proven themselves good hunters and warriors. He taught the young women to be good mothers when they married.

Anyone who killed or mistreated another Cheyenne would be banned from the tribe and could never again smoke the ceremonial pipe with the others.

Sweet Medicine taught the people how to choose their chiefs. There always were to be ten bands of Cheyennes and four chiefs for each band. Every ten years, the wisest of the chiefs were chosen to be Old Man Chiefs. They were to meet with all the others in council to make important decisions for the tribe. No decisions would be made until all of the chiefs agreed about what to do.

Chiefs had to be the best men of the tribe, and they were responsible for the welfare of the people. A chief could never seek revenge, even if his own son were killed in front of him. A chief had to always be generous to all people, even strangers. Whatever anyone asked of him – food, clothing, or anything else – he had to give to that person. He was to always be brave and to strive for peace.

⑤

The Cheyennes lived with the laws Sweet Medicine gave them for many generations, and as long as they followed them, their lives were good.

Just before he died, Sweet Medicine told the people a day was coming when new people with white faces covered with hair would gain power over them. They would begin to eat another kind of buffalo, a kind with spots, and their lives would never be the same again. When the white men came, the people remembered what Sweet Medicine had told them, and they still tell his story.

⑥

Fun and Games

Keeper of the Fire - A "Creep-up" Game

Materials for a group:
- blindfold
- 3 rulers

Play indoors or out

It was to an Indian's advantage to have sharp ears and careful, silent feet. This game is one way to develop these abilities.

A chosen **chief** is blindfolded with his/her ears left uncovered and sits on his/her knees in the center of a large circle of lazy **wood gatherers** (other students). The ends of the **sticks** (rulers) are place in a row about one foot from the **chief's** knees. Teacher begins by calling, "Wood Gatherers, we need wood!" and at the same time points to one of the wood gatherers. This is a signal for that person to try to take **one** of the sticks. The **chief** is sitting very still, but if he hears the gatherer he may reach out and tag the person. If tagged, the person rejoins the circle and the teacher begins again. The gatherer may not **rush** the chief. **Chiefs** may be changed after the three sticks have been taken.

Pugasaing - A "Stick Dice" Game

Materials for each individual:
- 3 stick dice made from tongue depressors

Play indoors or out

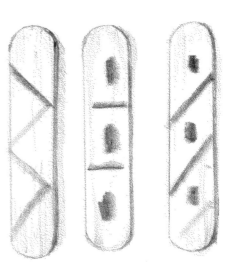

Decorate one side of all three tongue depressors with **BLACK** designs.
Decorate the other side of all three tongue depressors with **RED** designs.

To play, one person "tosses" their 3 stick dice onto the floor. The score depends on how the stick dice land.

- Three black sides up   3 points
- Three red sides up   2 points
- Two black and one red   1 point
- Two red and one black   0 points

Model a Horse

Indians of the Great Plains are creative and artistic. Indian children learn to model animals from natural materials. Beads, porcupine quills, earth dyes, leather, and wood were used.

Activity

The horse was a very valuable animal and changed the Plains Indians' way of life forever. Legend tells of a poor boy who wanted a pony so badly that he modeled one from clay. He treated the clay pony as though it were real, feeding it and stroking it, until one day his mud pony became a living, breathing horse. He became a hero for his people, because he had created something so useful and so beautiful.

To honor the horse's importance, model horses out of a variety of materials.

Steps to follow:

1. Wrapped wire can be bent and sculpted to form the likeness of a horse.

2. Horses can be modeled out of clay.

3. A large sheet of aluminum foil can be formed into a horse shape.

4. Create a horse form from wadded-up newspapers, held together with masking tape. Layer papier-mâché strips over the form. Paint when dry.

The Important Horse

Before the Spaniards came to North America in the sixteenth and seventeenth centuries, the Plains Indians had no horses. Having horses changed the peoples' lives completely.

ACTIVITY:

Draw a line to connect the ending of the sentence with the correct beginning:

• traveled everywhere on foot.

Before the Plains Indians had the horse, the people...

• roamed the plains most of the year.

• lived in large tipis.

• planted crops or gathered wild.

    foods for much of their diet.

• lived most of the year in one place.

• used large dogs to carry their burdens.

• did not plant crops.

• traveled by horseback.

• lived in small tipis when they roamed.

After the Plains Indians had the horse, the people...

• carried their burdens on travoises.

• caught large animals by driving them

    over cliffs or into corrals.

• ran right up to the buffalo to kill them.

Word Match

Choose a word from the word box and match it with its definition. Then find the words in the word search on the next page.

Word Box:

cooking pot	breechcloth	bridle
awl	ceremonial	headdress
moccasins	pemmican	robe
shield	tipi cover	arrowhead
parfleche	glue	bowstring
doll	ladle	scraper
sinew	bull boat	

---

1. tip of an arrow _____

2. tool for punching holes in leather _____

3. drawn tightly from one end of a bow to the other _____

4. worn by men and boys _____

5. used to steer a horse _____

6. related to rite or religion _____

7. girl's toy _____

8. worn only by chiefs _____

9. used to dip soup _____

10. worn by everyone in winter _____

11. footwear _____

12. container for storing food _____

13. made with dried, pounded meat and berries _____

14. used to remove flesh and fat from hides _____

15. used to ward off arrows _____

16. made very strong thread _____

17. required 14 to 20 hides _____

18. made from stomach or bladder _____

19. carried warriors across water _____

20. made from hooves _____

Word Search

```
K B A T C G D F E J K L I H M O N P Q M
J S H I E L D C B C O O K I N G P O T L
A I D P E U F G I H K L J M O N P Q R K
E N D I C E B A U Q Z Y X W V I T S U J
D E E C F G J I H M L N O P Q U A R S O
C W B O H G K I P O B Z Y X W V L U T H
A B D V C E G F C E R E M O N I A L G T
H U T E S B R Q P O I N M L K J D I H M
E V A R R O W H E A D W R A T T L E S L
A F W G H W E D C A L B D A T Z E Y X Q
D O L L O S N M P Q E A B C D E F P G B
D U T S R T Q P O C N M M L K J I E H A
R V B W B R E E C H C L O T H X M M Y R
E A U B C I D E F I G H C I C B A M Z O
S V L U T N S R Q P P O C N M L K I J B
S X L E G G I N G S Y P A R F L E C H E
P O B N M L K J I H D E S G F C B A Z A
Q P O U C H R S W T U R I B S V X N Y D
S P A O M N L K I J H G N F E D E B A Z
T U T W Y Z J B C A D F S C R A P E R O
```

Communicating with Pictographs

The Indians of the Great Plains did not have a written language. One means of communication with others was their system of hand sign language. Another was a system of pictographs, or picture writing, which was used on rocks, robes, and tipis.

Summer...long lines mean full-grown grass

Chief - feather indicates rank.

hunt

tipi

leaving or returning

flood

horsehoof marks

lightning speed

cross mountains

swim river

camp under the stars

deer

hill

bird tracks

buffalo country

deer crossed out indicates no deer

rabbit

symbol for day... plus lines to show how many.

lake

beaver

catch

meet

council fire

forest

dance

bear

feast

friends

stormy weather

rain

2 days

powwow

hike

coming together in friendship

award

surprise attack

war

feast

Write Your Own Pictographs

Rewrite this story in words.

_____

_____

_____

_____

_____

_____

_____

_____

Now try your own picture story.

Design some new symbols for your story.

_____

_____

_____

_____

_____

_____

_____

_____

Dressing Up

Formal and informal clothing of the Plains Idians had a very distinctive style. Daily clothing was without ornamentation. War and ceremonial regalia were highly decorated with painted designs, quill embroidery, and beadwork.

Wild animals, such as the buffalo and deer, provided the skin and hair used for shoes, leggings, and dresses. Wild plant fibers could be woven, looped, knitted, or braided into various items. Other plants were used to make dyes to color or decorate their clothing. Decorations were not only beautiful but often told tribal stories.

The following detailed descriptions refer to the ceremonial clothing pictured on page 43. The enlarged illustrations on pages 44-47 can be reproduced for students. Activity suggestions for their use are included at the bottom of the page.

Men's and Boys Clothing

For daily use a man usually wore only a breechcloth and a pair of moccasins. In colder weather he added a pair of leggings and a robe. Ceremonial clothing, as pictured on page 43 was much more ornate. This Cheyenne chief's feathered headdress would have been worn on special occasions—in battle and for ceremonies. Eagle feathers tipped with horsehair were fastened to a strip of leather that trailed from a skull cap, and fur tassels hung from the sides. He is holding a lance. Many braves wore single or double feathers in various ways. The ceremonial shirts the man and boy are wearing are made of leather, and are finely beaded and fringed with horse hair or strips of leather. They are both wearing fringed leggings and moccasins. The man's moccasins are beaded in a medicine wheel pattern.

Women's and Girl's Clothing

Women usually wore a simple dress made from the deerskin and supported by shoulder straps. Leggings and robes were also added in cold weather. The ceremonial clothing pictured on page 43 shows a Cheyenne beaded dress trimmed with elk teeth and leather fringe. The woman's braided hair is decorated with strips of leather. The girl's clothing is like the adult's, but smaller. The girl is wearing leggings. Both are wearing moccasins.

Activities:

1. While you read the descriptions aloud, students can label their own copies. Color.
2. Have students research the clothing of the Plains Indians and label as many items as they can on their own copies.
3. You can break the class into teams to research men's, women's, and children's clothing. Information can then be shared with everyone.
4. Challenge students to create a life-size model using the pages you have given them. Draw free hand on a large piece of butcher paper. Decorate the classroom and school.

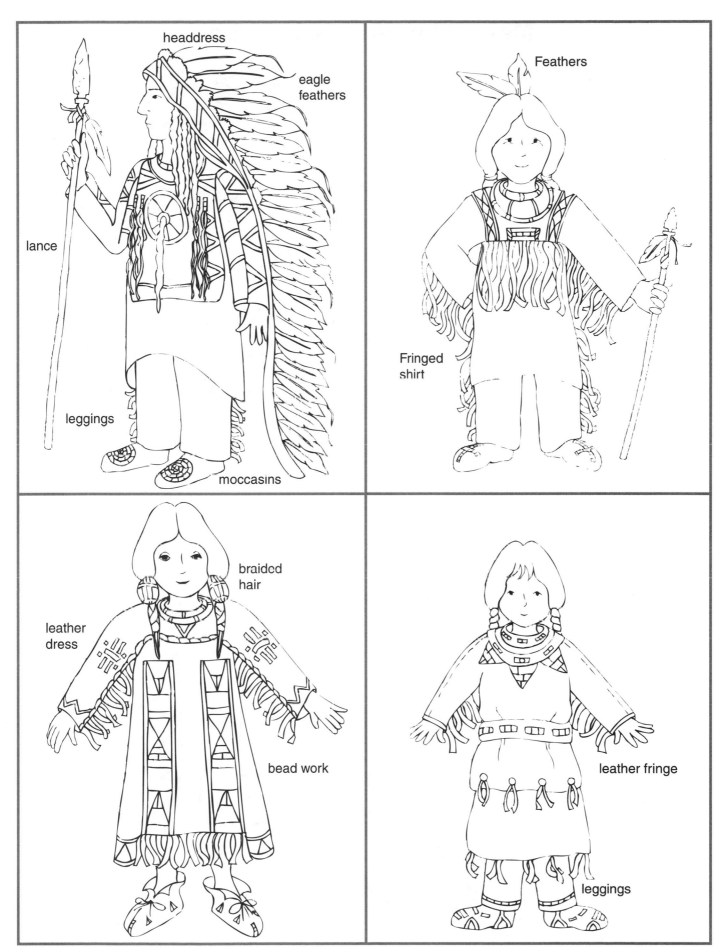

headdress

eagle
feathers

lance

leggings

moccasins

Feathers

Fringed
shirt

braided
hair

leather
dress

bead work

leather fringe

leggings

43 Plains Indians EMC 545

Men's Ceremonial Clothing

Boy's Ceremonial Clothing

45 Plains Indians EMC 545

Women's Ceremonial Clothing

Plains Indians EMC 545

Girl's Ceremonial Clothing

The Plains Indians Today

The Sioux live a modern way of life mixed with their traditions of the past. Many live on reservations. They still preserve their past with traditional dancing and singing. Life is not always easy. There are few jobs on the reservation and learning a new way of life has not been their choice.

About 8,000 members of the Crow Nation live on a reservation in Montana. They face the same problems of unemployment. In 1869, Chief Plenty Coup told his people, "Education is your most powerful weapon. With education you are the white man's equal; without education you are his victim." They have held onto his words and opened a college in 1985. They proudly continue to speak their own language and teach their children about their heritage.

Today the Pawnee are centered around the town of Pawnee, Oklahoma. They have been in this area since they were forced off their own lands in Nebraska over one hundred years ago. Many have last names like Horse Chief, Sun Eagle, and Good Chief. The elders continue to tell stories to the children. They are proud of their continuing heritage in the face of much adversity.

The Cheyenne have continued to maintain their traditions. They continue to call themselves Tsistsistas - "The People." Children are given an English name and an Indian name. They speak English and the Cheyenne language. They are strengthened in their daily life through the traditions that have been practiced throughout their long history.